Flashes &
Verses...Becoming
Attractions

Adrian Ernesto Cepeda

Andrea,
Thank You For
Your support.
VIVA LA POESIA)
Gracias,
AhEaa

Dedication

… to everyone who every sparked these solitary rhymes

I thank—
Mami for the gift of la poesía
Papi, gracias por creer siempre en mi
Michelle por la inspiración, my wife,
Las Palis for the power to poder,
todos at Antioch University
Los Angeles,
my familia, extended
et al—
las poetas, in my vida life.

Contents

Poems

The Sound of Surprise

When those cheeks expand and he exhales
his breath within notes, as his horn blows,
I almost explode, Dizzy with enlightenment.
There's something about the rhythm, the heir
of his playing, speaking with his mouth
and expressing such beauty on his canvas
of air, gripping his golden trumpet,
and all of the treasures he gifts us, even
when the vinyl is crackling back to the
Swing Low, Sweet Cadillac eyes closed
ears open, feeling the wind alone
as Gillespie takes us, each slight return
so adventurous, while reaching inside
his melody lingers resounding this cheeky
giant from his distance, sonically appearing
even as the needle uplifts us,
we feel closer to home.

Remember when Michael Jackson was king?

As the lights turned off
this was the day our class
stopped—to see him dance
the day we dreamed of Billie Jean,
watching his white glove glowing,
his silver sparkle gliding each
step a man moonwalking,
no one was talking we were
all shouting, the day our teacher
kissed the screen, leaving lipstick
on the TV, even she felt
with each move, gripping
that day the microphone
turned up his volume…
ovations more than standing,
from all that feedback,
that day we knew
—he was the one.

Estranged Fruit

Billie Holiday feels it
while gripping her microphone
unsteady, nerves pulsating through
her veins, instead of slurring words
she croons in the softest pitch,
her audience melts, gasping
in this siren's reflections
with surprising breaths. Their standard
pitchfork epitaphs are stilled. Billie stakes
her claim. Calming these beasts
stirring rhythms. The crowd devours
the blues tradition she slithers,
forgetting her own addiction and pain,
while serenading songs of love, every

night, she hides softly inside these
reflective refrains. Outside the Cotton
Club she is invisible, but instead she
smooths audiences with her voice
of beauty, adored by all who hear her —
their tongue-tied nooses swinging
colorblind for now. Putting their hands
together, clapping feedback chimes,

opening new ears while Billie shares more
boa, feathers—in the longest nightclub
dress, her hair held-up, uncurling style,
a spotlight of shivers— exposing her
roots. And they embrace true tones of her
every rainbow chorus key, inside this place,
Holiday rhymes a new sound of sweetness

she coolly redefines. Lady Day stuns –
lighting the stage without matches –
glowing proudly in her smokiest flame.
When Billie croons she can almost feel
the gift of her audience's embrace.
Bathed in applause of a lighter shade of
love, no longer caged—they can almost
feel her wings; on stage, this blackbird
rising in this roomful of doves.

When Bumaye was Beautiful

"The African crowd began to shout "Ali bumaye!, Ali bumaye! [before his fight against George Foreman]. Ali began getting energized. Muhammad Ali turned toward me and smiled."

— *Curtis E Mozie*

Still floating like a butterfly
from your red glove filled
with fists of love just ask
the Foreman, Liston and Frazier
side stepping in that ring like
a dancer, two step jab romancer
still stinging boxers endlessly.
We can still hear the bell
and all the raps from your tongue
and even Cosell's microphone
loves the rhymes of your charming spell.
And even the Beatles wanted to get in the
ring with you and not even The Man
of Steel could never destroy you.
And on *Different Strokes* the way you beat
the Gooch on the phone without even
landing a hit. And because the power
of your voice, gave to my skinny refrain

as I worshiped your Adonis frame.
As the camera flashed immortality
your battles were more than just a fist in
the face full of game. I may have stuttered
every other word but with every punch
you gave me courage to stand up
stammering words without my shame.
As I sat from behind witnessing
your sweating arms raised to infinity,
I raised mine when opening my mouth
spitting out rhymes like a stuttering
symphony. And to me you're still floating
like a butterfly and punching syllables
fighting to knock the world out with a
smile softer than Clay, echoing Cassius
like Jesus on the cross even in defeat
your bouts were my religion, even
in my tears you never lost; side stepping
in that ring like a dancer, two step jab
romancer, still stinging boxers endlessly.
And when I say Ali, still weaving
your bobbing head like a champion
as you mumble with greatness—
 "the greatest was me."

Re-turning Point

I see la niña Chiquita shaped like a banana
on the handle bars playing like me;
sometimes she calls me her dulce de leche.
She looks almond joy, like falling coconuts
unwrapped with skin of the sweetest café
sugar, stirring in a hurry, running so free.

Sitting together, we share the same
grades. Drifting off in history class,
these pages claim we are strangers,
but when I hear her sonrisa,
Chiquita laughs just like me.

She taught me la cucaracha,
trading almuerzos during lunch time—
when Billy called her an alien,
I punched this goon in the face.
Mi amiga didn't come far,
far away from a Star Wars galaxy
and the darkest side of an Endor moon.

Mommy, Chiquita's coming over to trade
discos. We want to go Platform shoe

dancing, and talk like telenovelas
chismando endlessly; but behind the
nodding, unfriendly look coming
from my Mummy's furious face
with the way I sound speaking in sí,
I can tell something is definitely wrong
but not with me.

Hanging Above You

I feel these strangers—
so-called art aficionados
exhibiting their inherit shoves
of selfishness just to immortalize
my love, as she's flashing down
below her so many demanding
strangers with iPhone cameras
instamatic lenses focusing
on her distant frame dramatically
fighting for pricelessly disposable
moments— just to catch, post, send
and redevelop this vision
that once captured my love
with what da Vinci proclaimed
was his *La Gioconda* sight. Exciting,
and so blinding, my love,
and she's not going anywhere.
There is no privacy for my love,
no time for powder, no makeup, no eye
liner, her portrait behind ropes, this
place where you could say
she resides, le Musée du Louvre,
I know she would love to break

more than bread maybe share
a baguette with me, my love,
and *un* bouteille d'eau
minérale avec du citron
to keep her widest exposure—
go figure. But she is still here suspended
in silence, my love, longing
for a touch of more than a stranger's
smart phone attention. So tight
lipped with so many stories
I bet my love wishes she could sell—
through this canvas on this exhibition
stage. Would she deny to truly
love the flash of devotion her canvas
smirk ignites? If you're lost in Paris,
come by and see my love before you
expire, sometime. Some probably know
her as the song Nat King Cole crooned
immortalizing, her face framed
and estranged to your vision;
waiting on your picture
to capture my love, Leonardo's
priceless muse, hanging
above you—forever enshrined.

His Strange Fascination, Still Fascinates Me

Like you
I'm an oddity from space—
a lad insane,
a scary monster
a super creep
who loves earbud listening
to let's dance while dancin' in the street.
You can also call me a rock and roll
suicide, this young American among
the stars like a Buddha of Suburbia—
I'm a still alive Lodger hanging
low tonight. How could I forget
my ashes to ashes? Like my heroes,
I'm flicking fame with fashion,
this quicksand Hunky Dory life
in this Suffragette city
sans regrets. As my iPod shuffles
Where Are We Now? This next one
is for my Bewlay Brothers: Joe the Lion,
Rebel Rebel and the Diamond Dogs,
Ziggy Stardust spinning so many changes

like Cat People putting out fires with
gasoline, pondering with a match, is there
really Life on Mars? Why am I afraid
of Americans? Time is a little wonder
like a Jean Genie screaming
over this heart's filthy lesson?
Let me loosen my Black Tie with this
white noise, share my internal
conversation pieces; will I survive
these . . . hours, like Kooks in Blue Jeans?
Bring me the Disco King,
this Starman will tell you: Nothing
has changed, everything
has changed; David Bowie
am I'm deranged?
Feeling unwashed and somewhat slightly
dazed—you, The Thin White Duke
told me to write this thirty-eight
line poem in a Moonage Daydream.

Not a Perfect Day

Turning up my boom box
now static, walking down
reeling out of tune on 5th avenue,
every *Street Hassle* lyric oozes your name
from every corner, my rock and roll heart
you would rip my soul with riffs
and then tear these holes apart
with rhythms from your bells—
ringing your understated rhymes
what happened to your journeys
behind those sunglasses? I would
hang your lyrics just like paintings,
your albums were my museums,
the wax of your sound
was my favorite kind of art.

You used to croon monotone
song stories, how your voice
would seize me,
shake me, awaken me
from my knees. How I miss

every part of your Hudson River

Wind Meditations, only
my dark thoughts could
understand; even the gutters,
high rises and exhaust fume
symphonies know it,
without my favorite poet,
NYC has become a wordless
wasteland as I spray paint,
Lou Reed, I Love You,
my message on this mailbox.
Who needs an uptown street map
when I can take the Lexington 1-2-5 ?—
with your songs I always understand
your verses were my favorite direction;
wandering without your chorus,
I'm still waiting for you— my man.

Stoned Immaculate: Jim Morrison Lies Here

I was the Lizard King and once I slithered
through my microphone cord. My leathers
are now stretched to squeeze tighter
inside this sonnet. Let me take you from
my palace, where I roamed in Paris.
The wisdom from Père Lachaise,
the cemetery where I once was laid.
Cerebrally electric, turned on, awakened
to feel unburied absolutely alive, wanting
to reopen the doors of perception but
I'm locked inside this confined rhyme
scheme. Feel me slithering plans
of disorder, start a religion of free verse,
seducing poetry with my Soft Parade, so
much harder to release The End, you knew
my lines keep growing wider as each loud
climactic scream grips my point of view;
exposes me long to be unzipped and
break on through.

His Microphone Eyes

Still flashing, Sinatra's ice cube reflects
her lipstick glass once stained half-full.
He remembers drinking her smooth
aftertaste still cold yet eternally stirring,
thicker with so much fire from her acid

tongue. The legend of Vegas went all in
with her flame, on every hand, placing the
Sands microphone on his chest— Frank
could still feel the confession's feedback.
Though his full house decked two of a
kind flushed with grins, the two
honeymooning lovers would play pretend,
but even with diamond rings,
their shuffling hands always folded in the

end. The glass from her once cocky bottle
stirs half empty now. The ice cracks, Frank
bites down, chewing time again, colder
now. The thrill still stings, ring finger
chilled, as Sinatra jingles his silver cufflinks
to recall the heat, when his black laced
feet could make her swing. He blushes

brighter with the orchestra tighter,
her sound perfumes; the aroma sends him
into the spotlight back to this stage
as Frank inhales her refrain that flash his
angel eyes, returning the silhouette
shadows of two lovers' flames consumed
by desire, glancing at the wings forever
fading… yet, their encore endures; in

between applause, his microphone grins;
the audience can see Sinatra sliding his
palm under his tuxedo, those wrinkled
hands pledging his heart—as Frank replies
softly inside each beautiful croon with
misty blue eyes that always remember…
she was my Ava Gardner.

Sitting in Black and White

On a London soundstage,
this camera focuses on his powdered face
trying to smile between missed takes,
Charlie seized the charming sunflower;
spinning her in his hands
glowing in circles like his woman in Paris.
Before reaching another
gold rushed idea,
his mind sparked twitches
like a flickering light bulb,
almost ready to switch on.
Chaplin concentrates
on this dizzy flower;
could it feel like riding
a child's bicycle?
Even from the rafters somewhere,
his concentration, close-up,
you could tell his eyes
focusing as the sunflower spins
reigniting inspired,
in a London soundstage,
legs crossed,
cane at his side,

glimpsing as the rushing colors sing,
within these magical petals,
underneath his spotlight,
blinking faster, tramping closer
under his charming spell,
Charlie waited for the laughter
to begin.

The Sol of Sinatra

Even the palm trees knew
to umbrella their shade
for this blue-eyed king
of the moon, glowing
icy smoke, while leaning
on Sunset…
Sinatra's fedora cool—
always melting
sunlight.

... easily, and I didn't[1]

How could I get over someone
like Marlon. He spoiled me—
whispering lines like an Adonis,
with a voice that mumbled proudly.
You have to understand, we
consummated that marriage every night
on the stage for many months, the way
we stared, glaring at each other like
husband and wife, we wanted to tear each
other's clothes off, and then again on
the film set that tension, never mention,
some nights I can taste him, that desire
still dripping on my softest of lips. I still
smell him—clean and sweet, dirty foul-
mouthed muscular baby—and I can feel
that back, the way he stood against
that wall daring me to take him, showing
so much skin and his mouth pouting with
such furious candor. So many nights I
wanted to bite him, I could feel him
teasing, coyly toying with me with his

---

[1] From a letter Kim Hunter wrote to James Grissom NYC, 1989

menacing silence. What no one could
hear was the way Brando would poetically
murmur, softly enunciating as he flexed
his tongue muscles muttering filthy pet
names, for me, as Stanley would, in my
ear. I could go on, and I wake up drenched
in that fire, wanting to take him
backstage with my husband sitting over
there but I carry his sensual smells,
Brando always lotioned his body up, I
inhaled his sweetest sensations, seducing
me his Stella, slow like a streetcar. I
imagine him crawling from the wood on
our stage, I hear him breathing, so wildly
naked with rage like a beast wanting to
get inside me and some nights, I didn't
fight him. Would you? Some days I wish I
did let him scar me with his beautiful
scent that way I could revisit his wicked
touch. I never had him and yet, I would
never beg anyone's pardon. We stood this
close as bride and groom; easily and I
didn't—I never got over his Stanley.

Looking at Her

*People had a habit of looking at me as if I were some kind of
mirror instead of a person.*

--Marilyn Monroe

She loved disappearing
in front of me. Changing
from one face to another.
She could be a sweet Tinsel Town
ingénue one minute and the deep
soft sultry million-dollar voice
the next. She sat in silence
among the clinking glasses
fidgeting with her near perfect hair
as if a camera had sprung into action,
while taking wild sips of wine
as if auditioning for a part.
Lighting her smoke to say, *Relax,
it's just dinner*. Rising again
she mumbled quickly
. . .*I will return.*
Checking my pocket watch,
I rushed to the ladies' room.
Knocking on the door, I asked

Are you still there?
Pushing in the door, I enquired
Is everything okay?
She was looking at the mirror.
What are you doing, love?
She stood in front of her favorite stall,
whispering: *I'm looking at her,*
like the way you glare at one of your
creations on the page. She is mine.
As if she was staring at a stranger's twin.
Softly kissing her hungry reflection,
staying beautifully present,
this is how I loved Marilyn;
clicking her fingers—
taking imaginary photographs—
posing with her always radiant wink.

She Returns Framed in Darkness[2]

"As for me, I am a watercolor. I wash off."

— Anne Sexton

I could never
wash off your scent, more
than water-colors my skin,
still glowing with your most beautiful
scars, wiggling underneath
all the places that you starred.
I can still taste where you kissed,
and the faces that flamed your touches
still strokes my secret yearning
so hard to hide the rise of my cravings
always concealing so much;
I loved your lips above me
canvasing my skin, brushing
me nakedly, palates of our
tongues, some nights I still
retaste you in darkness, each
gesture conjuring your texture,
your rhythms, your intensity my favorite—

---

[2] From Erotic Art No1 by Katsu Aoki Watercolor

always ready to exhibit these nightly
painting eruptions—your colorful
sparks, reaching with abstract
expressions to conjure your traces,
mentally framing impressions,
brushing your senses, your canvas
presence always reveals, imagine
your memory always wet, still
dripping softly above me.

When I First Kneeled Down

To taste her
under Rosa's favorite pink lingerie
as I would rub her grinning thigh
while feeling her up, I know
she could feel my instant hesitation.
Rosa's legs felt all prickly, unshaved
when her skin was like a cactus tree
she would whisper—
pretend we're in Paris;
during our secret dance, she hummed
the softest Sarah Vaughan tune;
I pictured the sweetest accordions
arching me closer enjoying each curve
from my Champs-Élysées
while canvasing her body,
Rosa showed me all her secret places,
rediscovering so much more than her hair
her voice was my map.
Wet like the Seine,
splashing much deeper, my face
licking up her sweetness
from so many layers,
now it was her turn for cravings.

With her teeth unzipping a favor,
remembering her glare, so sweetly
her hunger so intensely demanding,
but I didn't care; our mouths
traveled further, her lips softly
serenading, she inspired how
we loved devouring
each other, feasting our senses
each taste so enticing,
every space we uncovered
still savoring all the faces
we most decadently shared.

Guiding me from the Sidewalk

With your mom jeans rolled
up to your knees, wanting to
run off under the branches,
you softly unzipping, spread your lips
like we used to on the grass,
lick your bushes, feel you blush
grab your cheeks from behind
clutching your softest handles
I love to hold. I can tell you want
me to climb deeper, reaching inside
I can taste your thirst, from your
exploring tongue, as I feel you
whisper *let's forget the bars*.
Through the cold, we chorus
our voices, this time the Redline
covers our loudest tremble, as the train
rumbles by, you hear me falling—
gliding on top, loving your wiggles
taking me harder, blinking softer
under your tight blouse, I reach
to feel under your lace, so much
softness squeezing tighter, knowing
this is our last outing, remember

our Chicago winter? As the wind-chill
froze us, it felt so simple, forgetting
the wrinkles, blue jeans on
your ankles and our clinking
buckles, before the melting—
I still see you glow.

Her Moon Over Los Angeles[3]

I love the way she leans
   against the balcony
   teasing over Sunset
   Boulevard, Chateau Marmont
   showing off her beautifully round
   skin, ready for me to honor her
   cheekiest glow; before my telescope
lens angles… her close-up reminds me,
even astronomers at Griffith Park
Observatory would be focusing
their eyes past Hollywood signs,
as her sunset strips
and traffic down below
would try adjusting their mirrors
she shines so eloquently
already knowing
I have the most perfect view
our city of Angels; I wish
you could feel, from the balcony
as exhaust perfumes, how palm
trees bow their heads to this beauty,

---

[3] From the photograph Istantanea by Helmut Newton

as her fullest moon spreads
softly for me.

Destination Santa Barbara

She said, take me here
pointing south to her
wettest private beaches,
let's create our own waves
she whispered taking
giant breaths rippling under
covers, dripping skinny
like taking in the deepest
oceans as my salty tip
rises, I know she tastes
the splashes of excitement,
gripping her wavy hair,
feeling she is diving closer,
I tidal over from so many
back strokes— smiles while
pruning in ecstasy already
forgetting Santa Barbara—
becoming like the sea.

On the Balcony of The Signature

*"I like her; I could watch her
the rest of my life."*

— *Philip K. Dick*

As my best man handed me
a bubbly drink we toasted
clinking clear glasses of Cristal,
during our Vegas wedding
reception the way he pointed
to my love in white as she gathered
cheek kissing bridesmaids with giggles
while hugging my distant Colombian
relatives—at that moment, through
the brightening breeze, I whispered
aloud: *we're married*—The Signature
balcony had awakened me
as I realized at that moment,
glimpsing her within new light—
for the first time, this same
stunning beauty glowing
before me, I now call her—
my wife.

No More... Quiet Symphonies

More than just Vivaldi's strings,
play me so loudly, becoming French
horns and trumpets from lips—
a serenade of Mozart so proudly.
And what about cellos, between
her legs, longing for a bow
to spark the right place,
in the middle, even the last
note would beg reaching Bach
for his soft coda. I love all
the symbols crashing together
like metal bodies, Ludwig Van's
ears ringing in harmonies, rising
prelude before for the climax,
we can feel your hands conducting
the orchestra's last grandioso
breath, our exhales resounding
this grandiose of Mahler
Resurrection symphony
before the encore— Tremolos
in unison, more than a concerto,
bravo Maestro, for exploring
the energico faces

of our sextet epiphany.

We Couldn't Even Afford To Go Inside

I can still taste the air of sativa clouds,
in our loft apartment, as we spent our last
dollars on dime bags— joints rolled with
pages from our favorite novellas. Ivy
always refused to give up her *Catcher in
the Rye*, so I offered my *Sun Also Rises*.
She was more of a starving artist, than
me, foregoing any meal just to hunger
herself for inspiration. All I ever heard was
her stomach growling for leftover pasta;
I always brought home leftovers from the
diner— the place I worked nights to pay
the rent as she painted on bed sheets like
naked canvases.

We never could afford paper.

I remember the way she would draw
sketches coloring away on napkins in
between sips, from those downtown coffee
shops. Ivy would fill herself up with
caffeinated eyes to enliven her bong hit

highs— afterwards we would go wandering
around the library searching for new
adventures in pages. I still remember all
those books we checked out; we had stacks
of so many unread volumes; our books
would stay there like our imaginary pets
and our invisible children calling our
names through our clouds of smoke.
We just could never return them—

Just Kids was my favorite.

On other days we would visit the Art
Institute. I got my best ideas from Patti
Smith's book. We only had enough change
for one ticket, so one of us would go in
and film the art exhibits with our iPhones—
while the other one waited
and watched from outside.
I went to the Jackson Pollock exhibit.
It wasn't Ivy's style.
She claimed Pollock's paintings were
rainbow semen collages—
and I would argue, what's wrong with
that? Ivy would just sit there grinning,
her goal was always to get a rise out of
me, so she could get me to slip inside her,

again. This time it was my turn to go
inside; though I longed to share Pollock's
cum paintings with her, reluctantly
I entered the museum alone.
Filming everything from the inside,
I don't remember much of the exhibit,
but I do recall peering outside
and seeing Ivy across the street, bus stop
leaning while smoking another of her
hand rolled Bugle cigarettes.
When my cell phone ran out of juice,
I went out to meet her.
Ivy would always run up
and hug me, tongue first,
in my mouth like an airport greeting.

I loved the way she missed me.

I remember our last day together,
heading back uptown, holding hands
while she softly rested
her head on my shoulder,
walking closer to me, Ivy whispered,
blowing smoke against the Chicago wind—
*"I promise you, one day we'll go together,
and the world will be all ours."*

We never did.

Forget The Weight

Stop looking down while eyeing
this scale, why can't you face,
it's only a number and I desire
you in lace? Let me rediscover
your widest of regions when
you slip on those tightest
panties, feel me panting closer,
embracing your full moon
reflection—sparks the rising
and uncertainty of my only
up and coming attraction.
You always ignite me, with
your widescreen thighs. I love
you heavy, my beauty, I want you
like the *Abbey Road* epic. Can
you feel me, reaching for you,
with my riffs of desire? You
are my favorite guitar, long
neck and body so wide. The duet
of our conversation: your mind
is the rhythm, your voice the chorus—
I want to play your softest chords,
creating the most beautiful music in

between your thighs. All the skin
of excess you see, leading me to
your voluptuous palace, I love
to enter. I crave your sweetest face
when you lick the bottom, emptying
all the plates. Under the table, feeling
you slip off those heels, erotically
playful with your feet. Check please...
watching you shake so deeply
distracted by your beauty you
wiggle on repeat. Hungering
for more than your curvaceous
vision; dessert is my cherry on top—
spooning at home under these sheets.
With every kiss you forget the scales,
remembering with every lick gushing
your loudest pleasures unleashes
everything below your belt, desire
all of your wrinkles; simply, every
stretchmark I find, I must entreat—
with every thrust you love my touch...
enraptures me with your body
temple, seeing above me, worship
every love handle I savor with licks
hoping you finally feel me, of all
I suck—you taste so sweet.

Can We Spoon One Last Time?

Like our bodies felt the cusp
of your breath, ordering
your AM coffee, drinking
me up, all my darkest flavors
was your favorite caffeinated
climb. With every sugar spooned
like your lace and sometimes taking
it black when looking back, under
our table still day dreaming I can feel
your uncrossed legs waiting for me
maybe with extra whip cream
when I felt wet like the dream,
dripping so many licks tonguing
so sweet, how our lips defined.

Do I still stir you?

Sometimes spilling me softly
wondering my love, could we
spoon and maybe foam me,
savoring just one last grind?
Even Chicago reminds,
our neighbors felt the steaming

sounds and how I truly loved
how you tasted so divine.
Every last sip, I must confess,
feels like I am rediscovering
the flavors of every undressed trace.
So delicious, so hot will you grip
one last request, can we spoon
again in our most private space?

Leftover Bear Claws

If time eats the doughnut, does love eat the hole?

—Tom Robbins

A mouthful of Mocha crumbs fires
two-day old Dunkin Donuts
from her cracked mug—
chewing me softly,
she spits the same old after-bites
towards my glazed silhouette.
Her appetite hungers for a taste
more filling than my jelly flavored
crush. Staring chocolate iced—
I feel her aiming powdered sugar bullets,
softly triggering more blame,
leaving me shattered
like chalk outlines—
she loves finding a dozen reasons
sprinkling me into dust.

Love at the Soviet Kitchen, 1980

"Sex was never as neat as the movies made it. Real sex was messy. Good sex was messier."

— *Laurell K. Hamilton*

Forget that vodka bottle,
give me a sink full of your dirtiest dishes,
let me soap you up, scrub suds off
your grayest stained warm ups—
sans socks loving you barefoot,
the nakedness of your toes,
let me take you here

on freezing gulag winter floors
brushing aside our broken broom
as I adore your handles my love, feel
through your over-sized Olympic hockey
tee reaching your bra-less chest,
such a treasure I must confess,
to feel you like this, so unclean;
my favorite faucet wet dream…
keeping me awake, craving
Dr. Zhivago fantasies—
you can be my master

and I will be your margarita dream.
Let me stir you,
taste you with my cigarette breath
relight your nicotine lips,
tongue vacation after dinner,
not enough for dessert,
let me whip cream your hips,
licking every drop as you undress,
spooning closer
among the crusted utensils

of our rusty silver wear; as I slide down
your stained white panties, reaching
for my favorite part, licking off
all your saltiest sweat, hungers me—
why go out when there's all I can eat,
staying within me, feeling your candle
reignite, I love seeing your 'devour me
all my desert thighs' look melting me;
I can feel the flair in your eyes
undressing me with your lipstick
smeared look—
I'm already there, indulging
our priceless longings,
by taking down the ribbon
and inhaling all the beautiful greasy curls
of your unwashed blizzard hair.

Take Me to the Aquarium and Make Out with Me in the Jelly Fish Room[4]

Drop me from your soaked
and sweating pedestal
as I push your silver sterling cane
aside and put me up against this
antiquated glass, see through
my deflowered blouse that still
breathes your beaten name, gasping
while I salivate my favorite
of those plastic wrapped minty lips
tasting for you; me already netted,
our catch and hook reclaimed.
No more fowl mood, I'm hungry
for your early bird afternoon
special. I want to feel your drying
deviled tongue explore my still
wettest wrinkled sensations, sprinkling
of late December seasons tickling me
with your underwater shivers. Even

---

[4] after a photo by Dmitrijs Belokons

though your back's embraced I know
you can deliver. And maybe we'll rehash
us young by the waterfront Marlon Brando
and Eve Marie Saint like as you swam
dripping skinny towards the deepest
of my untouched regions, I remembered
you once treasured. Let us worship the
spine and tingling again and salvage
those now ancient across the pond
love letters sent par avion through
enveloping red, white and blue thoughts;
let me salvage those once longing
thoughts, we somehow dropped off
at the Salvation Army. I long to lick
your distant eternal fountain pen,
again, inked so divine as we uncover
instant waves, wishing your dog tagged
nakedness to reawaken me from your
symphonic nap; forget your fedora,
surprise me arising like a conductor
and I will string along your Hallelujah
chorus memory. Take me in this
aquarium, splash us closer, reaching
clenched, we will be drenched in smiles.
Watch the jelly fishes eyeing our pruning
wrinkles, seems so simple as shining skin
imagines us as lovers swimming

through tanks clasping our breath;
reminding us, to not stay in the shadows
as ignored background silhouettes. Let us
drool so much louder and they will hear
our once primal voices, roaring and proudly
now becoming redefined.

Her Eyes Hesitate...

I still remember serenading
her, the softest bilingual whispers
over her glowing wrinkled skin,
loving the body of her softest
poems as she scratches me
with fingernails while dangling
her keys, I can feel her
unbuttoning my fly, as I am
sporting my Iggy Pop tee,
she asks me while blinking,
will you be my Passenger, always
waiting for our next secret
entanglement— as our hands meet,
our touches conversing, Rosa's PhD
giggles ring unconvincing
as my belle accentuates her deep
southern reasoning— "*I promised
my Papa, no more poets.*"
She quietly mouths while
gently running electric fingers
through my unwashed hair.

I can tell as she blinks loudly,

she undresses me. Her fingers
like cursive writing
as Rosa slips off her heels
exposing barefoot—
her toenails painted red
as the pedal rests in neutral.
Rosa signals, keeps eagerly
flashing me as we steam
the windows while necking like
teenagers; she keeps leaning
closer, her shirt cut lowers—
I crave when her hands direct
me to her most delicious midriff,
I love when she wants me to softly
kiss all her beautiful wrinkles.
Knowing how much I live
for making our music electric
with so many sparks, she lives
for teasing me, playing with
the radio dial, no static between
us, she is already turned on—
her volume louder I stare slowly,
while contemplating chords,
intricate her guitar like memory...
as she reaches softly—
unfastening my seatbelt,
eyes flashing like spotlights—

I can feel the unbuttoning
of her stars.

Book Like My Woman

Although she tried to conceal it,
I looked at her spine first;
Like a library book,
she is often handled but never checked
out – never judge a paperback
by the front cover. Flipping

towards our introduction,
I like to feel, running fingers
up and down under the table of her
contents. I rarely gloss over her glossary -
Her dedications are equally essential.
Sometimes, between the hanging end
lines, are her most novel ideas— exhaled
meaning from her quixotic prose. Give me

the rarest edition, wrinkled ear
bent pages. Give me the anti-heroine
protagonist -No damsels or princesses
with crowns that never age.
I want to find her middle spot,
and dive inside, to unravel her
erotic subplots. Give me

the deepest climax and I will return,
over and over to her, my favorite
chapter. Tickling I love my tomes

heavy—I'm a hardback lover;
opening-up her pages like arms
embracing. I long to open her,
licking the edges and bookmarking
her skin by showing how much
I love her sweetest preface.

Living Next to Henry Miller

My Pops called him so vulgar
cursing our neighbor, saying
I don't like his type. All we
ever heard were the strangest
noises coming from his bungalow
sounding like Henry was more
than making but stimulating
loud earthshaking love with his
typewriter; I always imagined
Miller's fingers finding her softest
body on the page, pressing down
on the keys, each sentence had teeth.
Peeking inside of his window noticing
he was more than a book lover,
how Miller loved the glow
of the right spine in sunlight.
I miss hearing the music of Henry's
typewriter reawakening Miller's
most excited passages, making
his exclamation point, pressing
down softly with his index finger,
she even loved talking back,
craving the way, he pressed

down waiting for the ringing...
I could tell by the desire coming
from his hands, the way she would
answer at the end of each sentence,
more than in love with this writer—
Henry, definitely—was her right type.

She Is My Type

Every key resounds each letter
while engraving on my page
so loud, her expressions no
longer blank; no backspace,
no delete, when I press each
of her softest buttons, it returns
me to my favorite place, the body
line where I create. Loving
the ring, the zing of each key
even when I press down
it's as if she's evoking me
deeper, takes me back
to the time where scents
of perfumed white out's
widely ruled and when
sitting in chairs for hours
patiently, staring at her
metallic i's, our foreplay,
for each ink stained chime
feeding another paper kiss,
pressing down erotically,
ageless power, so electric
sans the chord, when

my finger touches her,
loving each feel as I hear
her metallic nails mark
with black ink; I follow her,
arrow keys, on this machine,
hearing the ding of her everything—
her tough exterior, softly she
hides her ribbon stains;
she owns my hands,
loving to please as I type,
holding the keys to her
most Royal space,
glowing from each tab
I perfectly place; she answers
me, between the sheet,
the harder I press down,
she responds —I fall.

Sandra Cisneros

I don't see a Mango Street house,
nor sounds of a silhouetted loose
woman splashing fire on howling
creek. I feel your pelo strands
long negro y caramello and all
the malo boys that tried to comb
you. I would never want to shame
your wicked, wicked days as I drop
el cepillo, pick up mi pluma—listen
as I flicker a match between these
stanzas hear me reigniting your llana,
honoring the volume of voices that call,
not tempting but consuming me when I
connect with your unrelenting corazon,
as I fountain lines you once enraged,
sparks within me the wildest gift—
your invisible regalo reflecting beyond
your cuerpo skin, libros tan finas
whispering to me glowing wrinkled
chapters, from your spine, my sirena
sage, I picture you ruling the ink
upon the brightest stage, let me
spark your closest wink, please

read and devour me, the last lines
I blush from my climatic page.

Carrying an Eighteen-Wheeler Refrain

"… here I hold your dream in my poem."

— *Rae Armantrout*

As he stands with fedora shadows,
we dream, listening wide awake,
gripping our souls with voces
hermosas resounding from
his microphone we are all
encantando as this poet lights
up echoing rhymes, repetition
ritmo, oscuro, tierra—breathless
our ojos y oídos following
as his words suave like jazz
musica his grinning keys
leaving us trembling with sparks
of enlightenment, under these luces,
he ignites our beautiful voices
simmering with anticipation
hanging on all his palabras, teaching
us how to make the salsa, savoring all
our idiomas y colores, he shares
the juice of his papaya poemas,

the fruits of his lengua
Mexicana. He speaks gigante,
fluidly carrying an eighteen-wheeler
refrain, from the stage. Even though
he's a different shade, I can feel
el poeta, he speaks like me, soñando
in metaphors, he even sounds like me,
with his hands in motion, swimming
in imaginación—his voz sounds
hermoso, echoing stanzas, poderosos
with his cuatro ojos, glasses radiating
fuerza from his fedora shadow, we feel
him beaming, he leaves us singing
our vida; believing palabras, echoing
our beautiful voices—he loves
glowing la poesía.

For Juan Felipe Herrera

Mas Poesias, Por Favor

The walls were speaking
writing verses for me
in different lenguas, labios
on concrete, making
sounds like the softest
nails spray painting
graffiti, fingers against
cement, calling of flavors
sensations of colores
like the lips from a lover
of poemas, licking wet
transfixed, my camera lost
within her tempting
translations, making
out verses using only
the exotic besos of her
gifted tongue.

Thank You Rochelle Newman Carrasco

When Tilting Her Head

"I have loved many women. And as they've held me close... But the only one I've never forgotten is the one who never asked."
— Renato Amoroso

I forget all that my Mama said
as we park, she takes me— breathless;
I don't want to breathe when she
takes our lead and miss a single
irreplaceable taste, electricity down
this spine, every snog like licking
books when I turn pages, this reclining
leather feels her, moves us backseat
with every suction breath she syncs us
closer, I can tell she is well read.
I feel her rewrite my favorite chapter,
I long to be her well-thumbed tome,
I want to feel her face underneath
my front cover, when tilting her
head, I wish she would open her mouth,
spread her lips wider and with every
poetic moan, just swallow me.

Thank You Sarah Frances Moran

She Entitles Benicio

She used to love the punk
poet, Henry muscle shirt torn
wearing tight, keeps his
heart sleeveless, hair gray
reignited poems flexing
words, his only prize. Now
she wants the silent one, who
mouths so many languages
to compose her, she loves this one—
who speaks only with his eyes.
The one on the screen, when
he blinks, he ignites a glow
so firelight, she sinks in her
seat, as the poet skulk's
loneliness his only shadow,
microphone echoes to spotlight
Rollins solitary rhymes as she daydreams
of writing new endings, with del Toro
as her starting role; unlike the
poet, she craves his spoken word
to remind, he'd breathe her
lines accented deep, inside her
ears Benicio will ring caliente

so sweet, creating volumes action
rising and denouement leaving
his mark entwined between end
lines— they rhyme complete.

For Kirsten Larson

Hotel Room[5]

And I miss the taste
of spooning ice cream
that melts, I still can feel your
taste inside my mouth.
I hear exhausts cars that pass
our room on the highway,
wanting you to exit on my
cul-de-sac, your entrance
is an engine that motors
loudly when you smell
my tightest of leathers,
loving to inhale— the wanting
you to unzip while licking
the gold glitter off
from my most private freckles—
as the TV snows, I sweat
in your favorite places—
hunched over pages open
to the part where bookmarked
so eloquently. Wishing you
would turn the doorknob,
rip off the silk tie, the anniversary

---

[5] From Edward Hopper's 1931 oil painting

gift, you love bonding my hands
with, to explore me, as your lips
reach for my hungering
thighs, dangling taste buds
you hold the key. Blinking
more fantasies, waiting
on bedsheets, ready and
dripping on sheets you
unmade with me.

This One Button Controls Her HD World [6]

Electric like her blanket,
she spoons with remote control,
pausing sadness that surrounds her.
With one button only, she can
pause her private world.
Rewinding frames of Thor like
flashback lovers—a Daredevil
story arch can make her blush.
This romance junkie needs a fix
of Jessica Jones as she presses play
to gush leather gifted tears. Next
week will find her closer to
reaching completion. DVR
excitement; her life is on hiatus,
as she reaches for her digital friends,
Defenders, Justice League, Avengers:
the strangers on this HD screen
are always there -- awake to keep her
company while her husband snores
through dynamic Luke Cage scenes,
Iron Fists flashing dreams, to her next

---

[6] From the photograph by Yvonne Griss - Woman Watching Television, Zurich 1988

cliffhanger climax. As her excitement
fades too soon, she wishes for a button
longing to control these emotional
parades that pass before her eyes
as she lies there playing back
her favorite lines, clinging to
Captain America comfort.
Superman bends her sadness
like steel in his naked fingers.
Iron Men strengthen her resolve
to reach her destination — Lost
like static silence, waiting
for the studio audience
to shower her with applause—
as the credits roll she returns
to her regular scheduled
show repeating the same untold
reality TV dream—pressing down
on so many buttons, she knows
the ending, she is paused and ready
to be loved, outside this plasma screen.

I Never Know Where I Stand

As another barrage of her
conversational grenades
goes off… with her aim,
it's either a black eye or
a bite in love within the heart
of our nightly conflicts.
Forget waving white flags—
it's war when she craves
the spark of our most
unfriendly fire, forcefully
showing all her pointed views,
cacophonous in number
smashing of her passive
aggression symphony,
screaming… *broken
glass is just like glitter,
isn't it?* I can taste

the familiar stinging
refrain of splitting up
again. This time not even
another volatile romp
marching to the beat
of her unrestrained wildness
would make up for her
latest verbal upset

offensive of: *you're*
in my veins you fuck.
Now I realize the reality
in her favorite tongue
lashings. And with my one
final bloody lip, sans her
nakedness, in our fox hole
lies the overexcited remnants
of another explosive love
affair, without the dynamite.

Loathing Harley

You despise the way she sits
upon. . . calling me her baby,
while she polishes every inch
of my skin, I'm always glowing
ecstatic, hard by her touch
magically, she holds my key,
and with her devoted breath
I grow metallic, god—with her
boots, she spurs me on, instead
of heartbeats, she loves to feel
my backfire. I am one, she's always
daydreaming of turning me on,
when she's beside you, closed
eyes longing to feed my ignition
and feel her cheeks so close
on leather, all you picture is her
riding me, swerving closer together,
even fully clothed as the wind
kisses us, the heat between her
body and my frame, no helmet
needed, she never refrains—

always returns to me at night

when you're drifting off, she
loves making my engine rev,
can you hear my roar by her
single gripping touch? Outside,
all over me makes her skin blush,
black leather jacket her body
armor, ready as she loves
to slide her helmet on,
foggy exhales her excited
more than alive with just one
glove touch, always loving her
seat the way she grinds, we are
always vibrating together
my Harley vixen more than
ignited while exploring rides,
even as I wait on the street,
while your asleep, who is her only
target fixation? I am the one—
she reaches for me.

Thank You Bernadette Murphy

No More Tears to Cry[7]

No words to confess
as she slumped her face
buried on my chest—
a familiar place I loved
feeling her breath
but at that moment
outside I felt nothing—
no excuses left. She once
saved accusations, setting
off in my presence—
waiting for her insinuation
to cause implosions
she loved untangling
best. The only stars
we saw in flights.
There were no other faces,
no friends, sans family
we never strayed outside
from under our covers
until the blinds showed
our shades, now we're

[7] from the Untitled photograph by Larry Fink, 1958

standing in black
and white. Sometimes
I think she'll miss my lips.
Our kisses always reached
for colors that never could exist.
In the morning the front door
was always open, the cold
would chill and awaken us
either she was leaving
or I was looking for exits—
despite each riff cranking
our AM solos before
the coffee simmered,
all crème without her
sugar; even our endless
cravings that stirred us
to rediscover this gift
each night unwrapped
we savored nakedly
and sipped together, remains
a consummation prize for this—
our inconsolable rift.

The Ashtray Said We've Been Up All Night

Although we clung
close nakedly
mattress floored
with lips and hips
locked in darkness
as our tongues flickered
reaching towards forever;
waking up, the morning
after, scratching the same
old skipping broken
record, like fading lighters
trying to reignite our midnight
sparks; although I thought
you were my muse,
as our radio returned
to static, how come we
could never find the starlight?

The Poets of Love

Stopped under the street lights,
looking up at his Orson
Welles like presence, she
glows like his Rita Hayworth
ink pink, starring in each other's
poems, as yet unwritten stanzas,
facing inspiration, simmering
half full, drinking midnights
together they can still feel
the jukebox ears ringing
from the pub's last call; riffs
signaling they're falling, dedication
shots toasted by lovers clinking
glasses, drinking up this spotlight
moment, thinking this where
she parked their car while
standing on concrete, their eyes
capture the elation of blinking
galaxies, together, somewhere
in San Francisco while
The Poets of Love glare into
their eyes— they glimpse
each other's stars.

For Allie and Brennan

Tears Don't Run Down Your Cheeks In Space

Still adjusting to the floating in zero g.
I just flipped a plastic bag of NASA corn
upside down, dumping out kernels,
watching every niblet soar flavorless—
atoms floating into the Cosmos;
just wish Neil Degrasse Tyson was behind
me to narrate my hungering hilarity. Time

is always hanging above, keeping me
awake. These lonely stars are faceless
angels, shining and eternally so moving
that even the paparazzi could never erase
the way cielo clouds and red desert meet
the ocean, naked bodies melting together
as milky chocolate cravings burns
into my famished mind.

Among the beautiful galaxy canvas
I still feel tiny and shallowly misplaced.
No matter how hard I pray,
My helmet hair dandruff clings
to this wrinkling face. Guess it's

true what tired eyes say...
no one can hear you dream within this
sleepless spinning. outside my window,
the universe screams silence. Why am I
always hearing rockets red glaring
inside my personal space?

for Reid Wiseman

Fear of Driving

Why is it when grabbing
the wheel, I immediately hear
siren sounds, attack panicking
my breath, I don't want to write
gun poetry and suffer another side
of the road interrogation because
of my caramello skin tone, like on
the night of my high school graduation—
stopped by SAPD, informing me,
my complexion matching the gang
description of some banger who just
robbed a house. I don't want to write
anymore gun poetry and raise my arms up
in the air praying to the lord up in the
overcast Southern Texas skies as I hear
my rights disappear with flashes of having
orange draped all over my hunching
back not wanting to sport the latest
style of new county jail jumpsuits
dreading confining me in solitary
and imagining headlines of my untimely
demise appear before my stuttering site—
all this appears in my head before starting

my car, I rub my Kokopelli Totem
Necklace that my poetic mentor
Alma Luz suggested I hang over
my rearview for suerte more than
buena, as I signal to turn into the freeway
that at times is not meant for me, mis
hermanos and members of my estranged
poetic family—retelling my reflection
I have no fear of driving—I just don't
want to write gun poetry sparked
by an officer showing off his own piece
and instructing me to lie on the hellacious
highway concrete, face down like a perro
in heat, just so he can check my California
ID, weapon pointing at my sweating

hands held up, while I compose my last
rights… to be silent verses as cars pass me
and my soon to be chalk outlining
my invisible skin as it barbeques, sun-
burning with humiliation on this expressway
interchange. I see myself seething like an
arrestee face down on I-10, not wanting
to let go of my pen fountaining, as
perspiration drops sweltering tears,
without any movements, suddenly
checking both ways…flashing forward

in my front seat, I defiantly compose gun
poetry; slowly signaling—I restart
my engine...so cautiously.

I Want to Feel the Choke in My Throat

Flags draped bleeding reds, right through
the whites of our blindfolded eyes,
like a cold that never wants to leave you;
grieving tears now censored blues,
color bar taps and keeps playing through,
detaching away from microphone
and evening news. The edited horns
from the airplane hangar leave us
wanting more; waiting for our invisible
hearts, all medaled in purple, our families,
our soldiers, now strangers finally
arrive to this place they called home.
Always, too quiet. buried deep from the top
storied newswire. Too explosive?
Why witness our casualties
from this desert storm? More
than sand in our cries, no need
to check the stats in the sports
section— we keep losing this score.
Too many lined up, faceless divisions,
fallen blacked out without national
attention, so much more violent,

with our forces armed, the end seemed
even closer than when we actually
disappeared; mirrors keep cracking cold
from the last words each private swore,
just like an addictive smoker keeps asking
with friendly fires, what were we relighting
for? All of this stillness through marches like
matches fading from the distance, still, no
one will witness, never easy watching
the breeze disguising this now disgusted
draft, once was so much louder, under
our muzzled buried caskets; must
this frozen outside feeling,
standing for all their honor—
fighting our silent coffin war.

Nature's Fireworks[8]

No rockets red glaring
just skies exploding
silence through natural
colors bursting through
dusk clouds, loving
to stare; as night approaches
taking mental snapshots,
I just focus on the glowing
above me, even before
the stars appear I feel
my senses flare.

---

[8] From a 4th of a July photograph by Gayle Brandeis

There's Nothing Like Gazing into A Campfire

Watching logs ignite, flaring to
listen for the charred rhymes
in between the flames
the fire pits epic poetry,
the wood refrains, hear
them yearn; as the smoke
rises skyward who needs a lightbulb,
your mind crackles introspection
ideas glowing in the nocturne.
There's nothing like watching
the most personal motion picture,
toasting without words. Your eyes
mesmerized as the sparks become
the most sizzling revelations—
there are no explosions, under stars;
yet there are poems sizzling quietly,
you can hear them stir, in between
the hypnotic interludes, where
nothing ever happens—
and everything always burns.

Cell Phone Dying Near Point Mugu

We inhale barbequed laughter
as your off key high maintenance
husband croons, *"I lied about being
the Outdoor type."* Campfire
choruses continue soaring into
the lifted Sycamore sunset;
through gusting branches, I fear
turbulent waves crashing, her salt
flavors tidal, calling me closer, haunting
me with unnatural claustrophobic
whispers keep flickering stories channeling
Discovery channel savagery of wildlife,
mountain lions, bears, tigers and not
because this baseball fan hails from
Detroit. Sweating to the all too quiet
and smoky stillness lurking around.
My sleeping bag footprints
simmer, ready with flash
smartphone light, gripping
car keys in hand, hearing too
many crickets mocking me
between the crackling wood
fire burning, wishing

for my wife to drive me back
to my static air conditioned, satellite
NFL Sunday ticket man cave
with voiced remote control; no
buttons here under the stars
to mute this sarcastic darkness
as I foolishly wait for one bar left
iPod to select my favorite *White
Album* Ringo "Good Night"
song. I shuffle some more trying
to find some bundled warmth
under this choking sleeping bag
as the cackling coals
of our serendipitous campfire
awakes me, again. Somewhere
this hunger lunges closer, smelling
marshmallow melt has me yearning
for s'mores as my tent dreams
linger. My impatient ghosts hover,
waiting for our exit to the 101
follow me back to my city
skyline direction, but not
tonight. I look up and finally
feel the stars, glowing
like a Pink Floyd light show,
earbuds soundtrack this holiest
of visions, finally, I exhale

taking in the sudden sleepy
calmness of my favorite
private moon. As Waters
croons "Time," I mouth
back unselfishly I can finally
feel new harmony— sounds like
nature brightly singing
in unison with me.

A Murmuration of Starlings

Can you feel the buzzing
   in the canvas sky? Sounds like
an etch-a-sketch of nature, see them
   soar creating so many shapes,
exploring massive wing like dances
   in the air— stirring my sight as I catch
the darkest figures silhouetting
   perfectly in daylight— glorious this
sight an exaltation of larks, exhilarating
sparks I feel my eye spinning
   my mind as I experience watching
their shadows soaring skyward like
   a musical ballet flying auspiciously
or perhaps these awe-species storm
   through clouds swarming together so
calmly in light, while silently snapping
   their revolving images
recapturing these murmuration of starlings
   starring above me. awestruck
with their flight.

Let Me Rise Up Like a Paper Cloud

"You see, some things I can teach you. Some you learn from books. But there are things that, well, you have to see and feel."

— *Khaled Hosseini*

I appear—
igniting fire
feel my flying, try not
to let the sickness
of altitude pull me back,
so much for waiting, watch
me flowing with this gust,
wanting to transcend into wings,
knowing I will not rise
instead become enflamed
as colors keep burning my skin,
so fragile and light—I want

to tear myself from this
place without spines
binding me, floating loose
leaf picture a once skying kite
descend; blazing faster
as the wind engulfs with

no land insight, watch

me soar flapping into brazen
skylight, as I turbulently glide
witnessing the spontaneously
combustible wonder
of my paper skin. Hearing
my pieces tear off as I embrace
friction dissolving me, feeling
Icarus more than closer—
I am his sun.

Raining Umbrellas

Things have dropped from me. I have outlived [...] lost friends...others through sheer inability to cross the street

— *Virginia Woolf*

Strolling in the French
Quarter sun on cement,
I see remnants of floods
flashing, branches filled
with Mardi Gras beads
falling as the storm
left so many umbrellas
on the sidewalk—
every step I take, I see
another forgotten soul
torn— left stranded
still dripping wet, some
unopened and waiting
to be salvaged, and
resurrected as someone's
cool cane or even a make
believe light saber in the grip
of a child, these castoffs
welcome any shade—

but as I walk I see so
many tossed off, I can
hear them seething
discarded overcast days
sweltering heat, broken
handling hard, just wait
till you need one, without
protection, who will save you
from all the thunder? Lightening
shimmering umbrellas holding
all their grudges as you're splashing
to find some Bourbon Street
balcony cover to avoid these
Louisiana summer storms, you
will be soaking with regret.

Her Only Light in Vegas

"I love you, with a touch of tragedy and quite madly."
— *Simone de Beauvoir*

Her lipstick-stained
Virginia Slim hangs—
ash seething but no match
as her smoky determination
exhales, still thrives even
while sliding in her last
crinkled dollar. No longer
at the tables, she folded
all her face cards of lovers,
now her only desire, planting
her soaked backside
on these wonky Stardust leather
slot chairs; thirsty eyes watch
her blurry hearts spinning,
while pulling the rusted sweaty
lever, even she is waiting
for her lucky 7 & 7 to arrive.

Tasting Her $100 Margarita

"Unwholesome thirst/ Stain my veins"
— *Arthur Rimbaud*

Simmering deliciously,
in the tallest glass, I can
feel this see-through beauty
calling my name. Her salty
teases sprinkled around
the rim, her limon lengua
aftertaste has me shimmering
excited with every sip of her
delicious Red O body, my tongue
does swim. After downing
half of her, craving more
than a sip, her two see
through tequila shots leaves
me thirsting to finish her,
I hear her teasing, "*salt me*"
tempting as she giggles
between each drink, "*explore
me with each drop;*" she knows
I can't resist her succulent
triple sec seduction, I know
she longs for another round—
to take me further and see me

falling for her intoxicating
flavor, more than just another
margarita this glistening beauty
always floors me, she must hear
how I adore savoring her most
stirring sounds. I know, we were
on the rocks, when I first graced
her icy beginnings; now I am
bound to keep melting further,
drunk with my taste for her
saltiness, there's nothing left
but her sweetest spirits,
glaring back at me, half-empty,
although she has vanished
from inside this glass—
more than thirsty, why
do I feel like I am the one
to have fully drowned?

She Pours Me with Her Eyes

Bottle aged, corked to
imperfection. The scent of her
filthy neck, tempting me; I crave
her...so, eager to take—
hold her by tracing
every inch of her wrinkled
curvaceousness; longing to sip,
lovingly and enshrine all
her sagging labels, as her
flirtatious thoughts
leave me unpeeled. I know
before even the first drop,
I will succumb; so thirsty
for her skin excess, I keep
reaching tongues, deepening
my taste; could I ever stop?
With every single pouring drip,
I undress her grins. She is more
than another bottle; I swallow
and feast on my own senses.
Her glasses clink... a very
good year. I long to savor all

of her, desire more body, flavored
aroma, I want to feel her glassy
round presence, my favorite shape
this aura so fine, her peaks I love to
handle; As I awaken her
uncorked experience, she repays
me by drinking me whole. I love
splashing our every last moment;
she becomes my liquor savoir,
her vintage aftertaste consumes
me... I need another drop of her
seasoned well lips; intricately
she sends me deeper, her skin
glows my favorite of her treasures,
my sophisticated temptress,
desires me; I feel her voluptuous
decadence wanting me again.
With every drink her flavors mouth
watering, and I am unbottled;
once more, watching her sink
back, all that we share and all
she gives me, her taste
swallows me, but she
always leaves me
thirsting half empty
and seems so much closer

then she actually appears.

Buzz Me

Anointed most requested
my barber Chau is an unmasked Marvel
without a cape. Power gripped
with his lab coated fingers—
not a hit man yet, he snips
like *The Professional*
but with the same silent dedication;
he stares intently
with blades in his eyes.
He's quick with scissors—
cutting like Wolverine
but with the grace of Scissorhands.
Our boy wonder is graphic, novel like
but he demands sharp razor responses
for my haircut symphony.
I listen for his music, like
a conductor with his sounds,
beautiful rhythms blurry at first
but I know as I feel the fade
in the back, jazzy grooves
on my temple saxophone dryer
blows on repeat—
as Chau spins me around

to face the heat,
my personal Coltrane
always cuts A *Love Supreme*
in this basement dwelling,
locker room size barber shop.
Chau drowns out trapper keeper
scat grinning humor with his electrical
magic as my hair falls—
misogynistic comb-over mayhem fuels
our laughter chorus—
this is last bastion for lost Angelino
Joe's bonding in gray areas
receding our comb over promises—
trimmed just above the ear—
conversations bent leaning
towards politics and X-rated mocking
knockers for sport.
No verbal victories,
My barber concentrates on his passion,
the hair before him.
Like Picasso he speaks with shears
the haircut is his brush.
Only the mirror reflects Chau's answers.
He knows, I don't sit for the testosterone
talks; I nod like a catcher
waiting for the heat, *buzz me—*
last week felt like a losing streak

I need a victory, I say. Already,
like my superhero, he knows, the sign;
No miracles man, I'm feeling invisible—
just resurrect me, this time.

Sounds Feel Trapped

"And the words get stuck … feeling cut off from everyone."
— *Britt Daniel*

My tongue trips with familiar sounds
like a wingless butterfly keeps flapping
inside the caverns of my raging throat.
This thunderous air won't stop gasping
with my vocalized disease, I am trapped
outside, arms flail, I feel myself stumble,

like an epileptic seizes with this stumble
humbling humiliation without sounds.
My mouth falters again, I feel trapped
as my lips like daggers keep flapping
spitting, teeth rattle breaths gasping,
every single syllable captured in throat.

Words like quicksand are jarred in my throat
my body jerks of a freak with his stumble.
If I could only speak, feel myself gasping,
nothing appears just stuttering sounds
like a cartoon machine gun flapping,
even my exclamation points feel trapped.

Stuck behind this podium why am I trapped?
This stammer rages inside my throat,
my lips feel like butterflies caught flapping.
My bumbling voice creeps with my stumble
Porky Pig made more gracious sounds,
far from cute when I'm air grasping,

I can feel the crowd gasping
for this invisible fool who feels trapped.
His lips cursing interference of sounds
caught inside my stuttering throat.
My body jerks I feel my face stumble
no words appear as my lips keep flapping.

Just mouthing words with some serious flapping,
coughing stale breaths, I'm nothing but gasping
my legs leap for syllables, I stumble.
My enemy is this Achilles tongue, I am trapped.
My words keep disappearing deep inside my throat.
These staring eyes deafens my stammering sounds.

This thunderous air continues gasping,
I feel myself stumble; my familiar stutter sounds
like a wingless butterfly flapping,
these words still trapped
as I keep stammering inside my raging throat.

Advice to Myself as a Young Poet

I give myself permission
to fall and slip on each word
I falter, embracing all
my fear. Although the tongue trips
in front of faces, strangers squirm
to my stammering, brings me
near to all the places
I stumbled embarrassed
from their laughter—
I give myself permission
to hesitate with my eternal
sentence, exhaling these gusts
of tension looking up
so surprised when I feel
their eyes upon me,
now I find my cheer—
with breaths inhaling
my own locked lip verses
plunging into darkness. Call me
the seer of stutters, just because
I leap with my words
doesn't mean you can feel
all the thunder rattling

never regretting the painful
ripples, the wrinkles
of my years. Standing
and still shaking I take back
all my tears, I give myself
permission to take back
the gaping toll of days
I fought when I sat
silently alone tripping
on my stutter step,
as I fell, grasping
nothing but air, embracing
each endless pause
while stuck inside
the climax— tongue tasting
all my fears.

Thank You Alma Luz Villanueva

Dearest Angelino,

Did I give you a hunger
for a shake while you were
floating, I jolted you
awake as you were
baked late last night?
Or did you really believe
you made her earth
move when you were deep
inside her busting
volumes, jiggling
with delight?

Don't worry if at first
you don't understand
the stuttering dialects
in my sidewalk talk—
think of me in Amusement Park language,
I'm like a Six Flags
warning of a roller coaster

but unlike that ride,
by experiencing me
on the ground,

will have you definitely
praying to a deity
you instantly rediscovered while
kneeling so profound.

Just don't get caught bungee
jumping or you might end up
hanging the wrong way on some
highway overpass;
and you might want to avoid
getting wedged in L.A. traffic,
and maybe find yourself
on some scenic freeway dive,
instead of getting stuck

after one or two jolts, you will
get used to my
trembling—
P.S. please, don't listen
to those skyping
end of the world
PC pastors who claim...
I don't seismically appear
because of California's devotion
for LGBT love, Mary Jane dispensaries
or Tinsel Town values.
Don't be after

shocked,
I also spellchecked
your Hollywood land sign.
Point your quivering fingers
triggering inside this epicenter
of this editor-at-large;
my name is San Andres,
and when you hear the sky is
tumbling you'll always know it is my fault.

Acknowledgments

Some poems in this book first appeared in the following publications, sometimes in slightly different form:

BlogNostics: "I Want to Feel the Choke in My Throat"

Coiled Serpent: Poets Arising from the Cultural Quakes & Shifts in Los Angeles: "Her Moon Over Los Angeles"

Drunk Monkeys: "Forget The Weight," "Hotel Room"

Ealain Literacy & Art Magazine: "The Sol of Sinatra"

Edgar Allen Poet Journal # 2: "Stoned Immaculate: Jim Morrison Lies Here"

The Fem: "Sandra Cisneros"

Getting Old: "Take Me to the Aquarium and Make Out with Me in the Jelly Fish Room"

Journal of Artistic Creation and Literary Research: "Raining Umbrellas"

Luna Luna Magazine: "Re-turning Point"

Men's Heartbreak Anthology: "The Ashtray Said We've Been Up All Night"

Nonbinary Review: 'Estranged Fruit;" "I Never Know Where I Stand"

Palate Poetry: "Carrying an Eighteen-Wheeler Refrain"

Poetic Diversity: "Book Like My Woman"

Poetry and Art for Social Justice: "Fear of Driving"

The Rain, Party & Disaster Society: "Dearest Angelino"

Rigorous: "Love at the Soviet Kitchen, 1980;" "We Couldn't Afford To Go Inside"

River Poet's Journal: "Advice to Myself As A Young Poet"

San Diego Reader: "On the Balcony of the Signature;" "There's Nothing Like Gazing Into A Campfire"

San Gabriel Valley Poetry Quarterly: "When Bumaye was Beautiful"

Silver Birch Press: "Leftover Bear Claws"

Sleeve Lit Magazine: "Guiding me from the Sidewalk"

Sling Magazine: "When I First Kneeled Down"

Spilt Ink Poetry: "Can We Spoon One Last Time?"

Subterranean Blue Poetry's The Children of Orpheus: "His Microphone Eyes," "...easily and I didn't"

The Song is: "The Sound of Surprise"

The Syzygy Poetry Journal: "The Poets of Love"

Thick with Conviction: "Tears Don't Run Down Your Cheeks In Space"

Tin Lunchbox Review: "No More Tears Left To Cry"

Unrequited: Anthology of Love Poems about Inanimate Objects: "Hanging Above You"

The Yellow Chair Review: "Buzz Me"

47-16's Volume 2: Short Fiction and Poetry Inspired by David Bowie: "His Strange Fascination, Still Fascinates Me"

About the Author

Adrian Ernesto Cepeda is the author of the full-length poetry collection *Flashes & Verses…Becoming Attractions* from Unsolicited Press and the poetry chapbook *So Many Flowers, So Little Time* from Red Mare Press. His poetry has been featured in *The Yellow Chair Review, Frontier Poetry, The Fem, Drunk Monkeys, poeticdiversity, NonBinary Review, Thick with Conviction, Five To One Magazine, Journal of Artistic Creation and Literary Research, The Wild Word*, *Rigorous, Lunch Ticket* and *Palate Poetry*.

To date, Adrian has over one hundred and twenty-five poems published in over a hundred different publications. One of his poems was named the winner of *Subterranean Blue Poetry*'s 2016 "The Children of Orpheus" Anthology Contest and two of his poems "Buzz Me" and "Estranged Fruit" were nominated for *Best of the Net* in 2015 and 2016, respectively. Adrian also had one of his poems "Longing for Our Airport Reconnections" featured in Shinpei Takeda's *Poems of Arrival for the Inscription Installation* Exhibit at the New Americans Museum in San Diego, California.

Adrian is an LA Poet with a BA from the University of Texas in San Antonio and he is also a graduate of the MFA program at Antioch University in Los Angeles where he lives with his wife and their cat Woody Gold.

You can connect with Adrian on his website: http://www.adrianernestocepeda.com/

About the Press

UNSOLICITED PRESS is a small publisher in the Pacific Northwest. The team publishes absurdly well-written poetry and prose. You can learn more at www.unsolicitedpress.com.